Partners in Preve

The United States
and International Institutions

COUNCIL *on*
FOREIGN
RELATIONS

Center for Preventive Action

Council Special Report No. 62
September 2011

Paul B. Stares and Micah Zenko

Partners in Preventive Action
The United States
and International Institutions

MIX
Paper from
responsible sources
FSC® C015782

Contents

Foreword vii
Acknowledgments ix
Acronyms xi

Council Special Report 1
Introduction 3
How International Institutions Prevent Conflict 6
Global Overview of the Principal International Institutions 13
Recommendations for U.S. Policy 22
Conclusion 28

Endnotes 29
About the Authors 35
Advisory Committee 37
CPA Advisory Committee 38
CPA Mission Statement 39

Foreword

The unipolar moment, to the extent it ever existed, has now truly passed. The United States is part of a globalized world, in which the flows of goods, finance, people, and much more connect us to other countries as never before. But for all the myriad benefits globalization brings, it also means that the challenges of the coming decades—be they generated by resource competition, climate change, cybercrime, terrorism, or classic competition and rivalry—cannot be solved or even mitigated by one country alone. Countries will need to cooperate on policies that extend across borders to address issues that affect them all.

In this Council Special Report, CFR scholars Paul B. Stares and Micah Zenko argue that the United States should increasingly look to international institutions—the United Nations and regional organizations like the European Union, the African Union, and the Association of Southeast Asian Nations—as partners in conflict prevention and peacemaking worldwide. These organizations can serve as a platform for developing and enforcing international norms; provide a source of legitimacy for diplomatic and military efforts; and aggregate the operational resources of their members, all of which can increase the ease and effectiveness of American peacemaking efforts.

The CSR explores the ways these institutions are already contributing to the creation and maintenance of peace, from the UN's conflict monitoring systems to the dispute resolution mechanisms at the Organization of American States and the nascent African Standby Force of the African Union, before turning to a series of recommendations on ways the United States can improve its interaction with these institutions and maximize their potential.

To reduce the risk of conflict, the authors write, the United States should work to expand and institutionalize international norms against both intra- and interstate violence. They also suggest that the United States further efforts toward economic growth and good governance in the developing world, both of which reduce the potential for conflict, and work to institutionalize a limited form of the responsibility to protect. To head off brewing conflicts, the authors recommend closer cooperation among the United States and international institutions on conflict monitoring and intelligence sharing, coordination on aid disbursements, and increasing American representation on and funding to bodies working in these areas. And where conflict has already broken out, they note, the United States could still enable a rapid response by enhancing international capacity to quickly deploy civilian and military assets to new conflict zones.

Partners in Preventive Action raises important issues for U.S. policymakers contemplating a world of increasing complexity at a time of decreasing means. It provides a comprehensive look at the conflict prevention capacity of international institutions and poses thoughtful recommendations on how they can be improved. While there will continue to be a place for independent action, ad hoc coalitions, and formal alliances, this CSR successfully argues for the present and future importance of international institutions.

Richard N. Haass
President
Council on Foreign Relations
September 2011

Acknowledgments

This report complements our earlier Council Special Report *Enhancing U.S. Preventive Action*, published in 2009. We thank CFR President Richard N. Haass and Director of Studies James M. Lindsay for supporting this project and for providing helpful comments from its inception.

As is typical, this report is the product of people giving generously of their time and expertise from start to finish. In particular, we benefited enormously from the advisory committee that met on two occasions and that also individually provided invaluable comments along the way. We would like to single out Nancy Soderberg, who chaired the committee, along with John Campbell, Michèle Griffin, David A. Hamburg, Matthew L. Hodes, Kara C. McDonald, Yadira Soto, Joanna Weschler, and Lawrence S. Woocher. In addition, dozens of officials from the U.S. government, the United Nations, and several regional organizations provided invaluable insights and recommendations that greatly contributed to the quality of the report.

Finally, we are grateful to Patricia Dorff and Lia Norton in Publications for their terrific guidance and editing support and to Lisa Shields, Leigh-Ann Krapf Hess, Lucy Dunderdale, and Melinda Brouwer in Communications and Marketing for working to promote and distribute the report. We also appreciate the contributions of Program Associate Andrew Lim and Studies Administrator Kate Howell for guiding the CSR through the Studies process, and the tireless logistical, research, and intellectual support of former and current CPA staff members Elise Vaughan, Rebecca Friedman, Andrew Miller, Stephen Wittels, Sophia Yang, and Emma Welch.

This publication was made possible by a grant from the Carnegie Corporation of New York. CFR also expresses its thanks to the Robina Foundation for its support for Micah Zenko's work on multilateral dimensions of conflict prevention. The statements made and views expressed herein are solely our own.

Paul B. Stares
Micah Zenko

Acronyms

ASEAN	Association of Southeast Asian Nations
AU	African Union
CFSP	Common Foreign and Security Policy
DPA	United Nations Department of Political Affairs
DPKO	United Nations Department of Peacekeeping Operations
ECOWAS	Economic Community of West African States
ESDP	European Security and Defense Policy
EU	European Union
G8	Group of Eight
G20	Group of Twenty
GCC	Gulf Cooperation Council
ICC	International Criminal Court
IFI	international financial institution
IMF	International Monetary Fund
NATO	North Atlantic Treaty Organization
OAS	Organization of American States
OECD	Organization for Economic Cooperation and Development
OSCE	Organization for Security and Cooperation in Europe
P5	five permanent members of the United Nations Security Council
R2P	responsibility to protect
UN	United Nations
USAID	U.S. Agency for International Development

Council Special Report

Introduction

With the U.S. military overstretched after a decade of continuous combat operations and Washington facing acute fiscal pressures, the strategic logic of preventive action to reduce the number of foreign crises and conflicts that could embroil the United States in burdensome new commitments has never been more compelling.[1]

Yet reducing violent conflict around the world is not a task that the United States can or should take on alone; the magnitude and complexity of emerging challenges to international peace and stability are too great and their potential impact too far-reaching. Although large-scale deadly conflicts have markedly diminished—interstate war is rare and civil wars have declined since the mid-1990s—this trend may not last. The twenty-first century poses many dangers: growing friction between rising and established powers, the diffusion of deadly technologies (including to nonstate actors), mounting economic and social pressures aggravated by demographic trends, resource scarcities, and climate change could all markedly increase the incidence of violent conflict. If these threats materialize, no country is likely to be spared the consequences; the world is simply too interconnected. Preventing deadly conflict has to be a shared imperative and responsibility.

International preventive action offers a solution to this problem. It can be pursued through informal ad hoc arrangements or formal multilateral organizations such as the United Nations, various regional bodies, and international financial institutions (IFIs). Though many Americans remain uninformed or skeptical about the value of international organizations, particularly in helping to prevent deadly conflict, the organizations provide important benefits over purely unilateral or informal efforts. Every U.S. administration since the founding of the United Nations—even the supposedly unilateralist George W. Bush administration—has recognized these benefits and utilized international organizations to promote peace and security.

Three critical attributes of international organizations stand out:

- They offer an institutional platform for formalizing, extending, and at times enforcing international rules, norms, and regimes that regulate state behavior and make the international environment more orderly and predictable. For the most part, the United States has been able to shape and promote international rules and norms that embody American values and goals.

- International organizations' endorsements provide an important source of legitimacy to diplomatic efforts initiated or supported by the United States. This backing is especially useful when such efforts involve breaching the otherwise sacrosanct principle of noninterference in the internal affairs of another state. Securing a multilateral organization's imprimatur helps unlock assistance from the organization's member states and can be critical for sustaining domestic support.

- International organizations have significant operational benefits, such as information on and operational access to parts of the world, that may be hard for the United States to obtain independently. To the extent that the success of conflict prevention initiatives rests on either extending or withholding certain goods and services to influence the behavior of recalcitrant states, the active involvement of international organizations is often indispensable. Even when it is not, using an international organization's resources is often more cost-effective for the United States than unilateral action.

While informal arrangements like the Group of Eight (G8) or Group of Twenty (G20), not to mention ad hoc "coalitions of the willing," can complement the work of established formal institutions, they lack the legitimacy derived from their standing in international law and their broad, sometimes universal, membership. More importantly, with little or no staff and infrequent meetings, informal institutions' ability to prevent conflict is limited. They do not have the experienced diplomatic and military capacity of international institutions and frequently require the United Nations (UN) or regional bodies to mandate and actually carry out preventive action.

By actively improving the ability of the leading international institutions to carry out conflict prevention, the United States will have more effective partners in instances where it has a major stake and will find less need for involvement where it does not. That said, U.S. efforts to enhance international capacity for preventive action must be based on a clear-eyed assessment of the strengths and weaknesses of the leading multilateral actors. Before turning to a brief global overview of the leading international institutions, it is important to first understand how they help prevent violent conflict.

How International Institutions Prevent Conflict

Formal international institutions contribute to the prevention of deadly conflict in ways that are not always easy to demonstrate in a precise fashion. This is because violent conflict can manifest itself in many forms for many different reasons. Efforts to prevent and control conflict, therefore, typically entail multifaceted policy interventions with results that may not be immediately apparent or easy to evaluate individually for their relative effectiveness. Proving that policy y or initiative x averted a conflict—that is, prevented an event from happening—ultimately rests on an irresolvable counterfactual argument. However, from observed changes in the type and incidence of armed conflict over time, as well as more immediate indicators that a particular policy initiative or intervention has helped halt a deteriorating or escalating situation, it is possible to infer the impact of deliberate prevention efforts. To understand better the role of international institutions in preventing violent conflict, it is useful to divide their involvement into three broad categories: conflict risk reduction, crisis prevention, and conflict mitigation measures.[2]

CONFLICT RISK REDUCTION

There are measures taken to minimize potential sources of instability and conflict before they arise. They encompass, on the one hand, efforts to reduce the impact of specific threats, such as controlling the development of destabilizing weapon systems or arms transfers that may cause regional power imbalances; restricting the potential influence of dangerous nonstate actors; and diminishing the possible negative impact of anticipated demographic, economic, and environmental change. On the other hand, they cover measures that promote conditions conducive to peace and stability. Within states, these include encouraging equitable economic development, good governance, the rule of law, and respect for human rights, and between them, stability can be enhanced through rules on the use of force, military and economic cooperation, security guarantees, confidence-building measures, functional integration, and effective arbitration mechanisms, among other things.

International organizations help foster and implement most, if not all, of these risk-reduction efforts. At the most fundamental level, they set and reinforce basic rules and norms of responsible state behavior that make the world less anarchical. The UN Charter is paramount in this regard. Increasingly, those norms and rules apply to how states behave internally toward their citizens. Most notably, the mandate to protect civilians—often referred to as the "responsibility to protect" (R2P) norm—has gained increasing traction. From the late 1990s onward, a growing number of UN-sanctioned actions has been explicitly mandated to protect civilians threatened by mass violence, most recently with regard to Libya.[3] All UN member states' adoption of the R2P provisions at the 2005 World Summit bolstered the standing of this emerging norm, which explicitly obliges states to protect their populations from genocide, war crimes, ethnic cleansing, and crimes against humanity and, moreover, calls on the international community—meaning the UN and regional organizations—to take collective action if states fail to do so.[4] Over the same period, the International Criminal Court (ICC), established in 1998 to indict and convict individuals of war crimes and crimes against humanity, has provided a venue for legal enforcement of R2P. Declarative endorsements of R2P by various regional organizations and, in the notable case of the African Union (AU), incorporation of it into its founding charter, have contributed further to its status as an accepted global norm.[5]

Besides these normative advances, international institutions help foster political cooperation and economic development that over time bring greater trust and transparency to interstate relations. In particular, their mechanisms for settling disputes peacefully and the incentives they provide for collective over individual action have deepened the level of functional if not political integration to make interstate war increasingly irrational and obsolete. The European Union (EU) is clearly the best example of how an international institution has evolved to make war virtually unthinkable in Europe. A desire for peace and stability undoubtedly provided the prior conditions for the EU's creation, but the increasingly dense set of interdependent relationships it engendered has reinforced the underlying imperative. The Organization of American States (OAS) has also succeeded at creating effective legal mechanisms and promoting norms of noninterference that have made interstate wars rare among member states and prevented the escalation of boundary disputes.

Buttressing these efforts is the role that international institutions play in helping constrain the world's most destabilizing weapon systems through numerous international agreements—notably the Nuclear Nonproliferation Treaty, the Comprehensive Test Ban Treaty, the Chemical Weapons Convention, and the Biological Weapons Convention—which by extension lessen the risk of war. These agreements also require international organizations to manage and monitor compliance.

As violent conflict has become largely confined within state borders, international organizations have increasingly turned their attention to reducing the risk factors associated with weak, failing, and ultimately violently unstable states. These include ineffectual or corrupt political and financial institutions, feeble economic performance, poor mortality and health indicators, resource scarcities, and inadequate judicial and police structures. The UN and many regional organizations, as well as international financial institutions such as the World Bank, International Monetary Fund (IMF), and regional development banks, now all actively promote democratic governance, the rule of law, and sustainable economic development to lessen the risk of civil conflict without necessarily labeling them conflict prevention efforts.[6] Because the IFIs are not overtly political organizations, states typically view them as less intrusive and are thus more accepting of IFI monitoring, analytical functions, and missions.

Finally, international institutions contribute in numerous ways toward tackling illicit economic activities, including the drug trade, human trafficking, counterfeiting, and the extraction of conflict minerals that can also facilitate armed conflict. These efforts have had a demonstrable effect in specific conflict-afflicted areas, if not yet globally.

CRISIS PREVENTION

Crisis prevention initiatives are taken in anticipation that relations between two states or the situation within a country could deteriorate dangerously and devolve into violent conflict. A host of diplomatic, military, economic, and legal measures can be employed preemptively to remove or minimize potential triggers of a crisis or alter the decision calculus of the parties to the potential conflict. These can include cooperative initiatives (such as diplomatic persuasion and mediation, economic assistance and incentives, legal arbitration, and military support) as well as coercive instruments (diplomatic condemnation and isolation, various economic sanctions, legal action, preventive military deployments, and threats of punitive action).

Such early interventions to prevent crises have traditionally not been the strong suit of international organizations. Generating the necessary consensus for collective preventive action is hard when member states typically have different interests at stake and differing assessments of the likelihood of violent conflict. However, as the UN and some regional organizations have had to bear the enormous burdens associated with postconflict stabilization and reconstruction, they have quietly increased their efforts in early prevention through discreet diplomatic means—that is, quiet diplomacy—and other activities not typically viewed as conflict prevention. These preventive efforts have been effective in several areas.

– *Electoral processes/political transitions:* Elections and other political transitions are particularly prone to producing violence, as demonstrated in places as diverse as Algeria, Burundi, Kenya, Nepal, Haiti, Sri Lanka, and, most recently, the Ivory Coast.[7] The UN and regional organizations like the EU, the Organization for Security and Cooperation in Europe (OSCE), and the OAS provide pre-electoral technical assistance and monitoring to help facilitate violence-free elections and to deter improprieties. Preventive efforts were reportedly successful in recent years in the Solomon Islands (2010); Lesotho and Madagascar (2009); Ghana, Kenya, and the Maldives (2008); and Mauritania and Sierra Leone (2007).[8] Postelection international endorsement of the process can enhance the winner's legitimacy or lay the basis for economic or diplomatic penalties for fraudulent elections. Quiet mediation by international organizations' representatives, often in conjunction with an informal coalition of countries, can also help dissuade civilian or military leaders from taking extra-constitutional political actions. In 2010, the UN's Office for West Africa successfully encouraged military leaders in Guinea, Togo, and Niger to fulfill their commitments to transfer power to civilian authorities. The UN also lends its substantial experience in crafting new constitutions during tense political transitions, as in Kyrgyzstan following the ouster of its president in 2010.

– *Ethnic/religious frictions*: International actors often work quietly to defuse tensions between different ethnic or religious communities or redress the grievances of specific minority groups before they erupt into violence. A notable example has been the work of the OSCE's high commissioner for minorities in addressing the discrimination toward ethnic groups in eastern and central Europe—a historical source of violent unrest and secessionist pressures. Similar preventive efforts by the EU and the UN Assistance Mission for Iraq have focused on Kosovo and the city of Kirkuk in Iraq's Kurdish region.

– *Boundary/territorial disputes:* International organizations have long played a role in arbitrating land and maritime borders disputes. In 2010, the UN's International Court of Justice worked with the UN's Office for West Africa to adjudicate a tense border dispute—exacerbated by the discovery of oil deposits—involving Cameroon and Nigeria. The UN's Regional Center for Preventive Diplomacy for Central Asia has achieved success in resolving water rights issues in the region. Likewise, the OAS successfully mediated a border dispute between Belize and Guatemala, while the Association of Southeast Asian Nations (ASEAN) has served as a broker and observer for the long-standing border conflict between Cambodia and Thailand. With increasing pressure on resources and newly accessible areas opening to exploitation, preventive boundary/territorial dispute resolution will assume greater importance.

– *Resource/food scarcities:* International organizations are becoming better at anticipating how certain shocks such as price spikes, food shortages, or natural disasters can trigger political unrest and violence. Both the World Bank and the IMF have recently taken important steps to stem these developments through such initiatives as contingent emergency loans and flexible credit lines. The UN's World Food Program created and operates the Inter-Agency Standing Committee on Humanitarian Early Warning Service, which provides easily accessible humanitarian early warnings and forecasts for the natural hazards that often precede food shortages.

– *Special investigations*: The UN and some regional organizations are increasingly conducting special investigations of potentially destabilizing events in countries where the capacity or impartiality of the government is questioned. Recent examples include the UN investigation into the 2005 assassination of Lebanese prime minister Rafik Hariri, a joint UN–Economic Community of West African States (ECOWAS) fact-finding inquiry into the deaths of Ghanaian migrants in Gambia in 2007, an investigation of human rights violations at the end of the Sri Lankan civil war in 2009, and an independent panel of inquiry into the Israeli raid on the flotilla of ships carrying aid to Gaza in 2010.

CONFLICT MITIGATION

Should earlier preventive efforts fail to have the desired effect or violence erupt with little or no warning, many of the same basic measures and techniques can be employed to manage and mitigate the crisis. These include efforts targeted at the parties to a conflict to facilitate cooperative dispute resolution and change their incentive structures to promote peaceful outcomes. Thus steps can be taken to identify and empower "moderates," isolate or deter potential "spoilers," and sway the uncommitted. More interventionist measures to protect endangered groups or secure sensitive areas through such tactics as observer missions, arms embargoes (or arms supplies), and preventive military or police deployments are also conceivable. Of potential equal importance in some circumstances, moreover, are the preventive initiatives to help contain a relatively localized crisis or flash point to help ensure the conflict does not either spread or draw in others. Indeed, containment may realistically be the only crisis mitigation option.

The UN and regional organizations have on many occasions carried out conflict mitigation efforts. Being generally perceived as impartial or neutral actors certainly helps in allowing them to broker negotiated compromises, offer their "good offices," and serve as third-party mediators and arbitrators. And, given the collective influence of their membership, international organizations have advantages in threatening and imposing coercive measures such as economic sanctions, travel restrictions, and arms embargoes. They also have the added benefit of being able to legitimize such actions, something individual states and even informal coalitions have difficulty doing. This is not to suggest, however, that international conflict mitigation efforts are uncontroversial and straightforward. At the UN Security Council, the veto-wielding five permanent (P5) members effectively determine which conflicts the organization focuses on; not surprisingly, these typically involve small and medium-sized powers. The same is true of intrastate conflicts; cases internal to or involving one of the P5 are generally off limits. A similar dynamic plays out within the principal regional peace and security organizations, though as the capacities of these organizations grow they are becoming more apt to fill the vacuum created by P5 disagreements.[9]

Global Overview of the Principal International Institutions

UNITED NATIONS

As the only international organization with a global mandate to prevent and resolve armed conflict, the UN has the most established set of arrangements, deployable assets, and qualified personnel for this purpose. Since the early 1990s, these capacities have expanded, albeit in a halting fashion, despite member states' reservations about enabling an intrusive UN apparatus.[10] The resulting assortment of informal "work-around" arrangements is neither ideal nor efficient, but as one 2010 official report concluded, the UN system "does not lack relevant information," and "substantial progress has been made over the past decade in enhancing United Nations early warning capacities."[11]

Ongoing efforts to make use of this early-warning information are driven by the UN's Department of Political Affairs (DPA), which produces analytical reports and briefing notes warning of incipient crises for its director—the undersecretary-general for political affairs—and transmits information to the UN's Executive Committee on Peace and Security.[12] The undersecretary-general also participates in the secretary-general's policy committee, "a cabinet-style decision-making mechanism" that provides strategic guidance to the secretariat.[13] In addition, the undersecretary-general can report warnings of potential conflict directly to the secretary-general, who can raise matters informally with Security Council members at monthly working lunches, or formally through the council's scheduled work program.

DPA works closely with the UN Development Program, and in particular its Bureau of Crisis Prevention and Recovery, to manage the UN's informal interagency coordination mechanism—the UN Framework for Coordination on Preventive Action (i.e., the Framework Team).[14] Both departments, moreover, are increasingly engaged in early, on-the-ground prevention efforts through their missions overseas. DPA, in particular, has recently become more operational, with thirteen field missions around the world engaged in a variety of activities involving electoral assistance, facilitated dialogues through their "good offices," and quiet mediation efforts.[15] In the event of a serious and unexpected crisis, both departments have a modest capacity to bolster existing missions or send officials on new assignments. In 2006, DPA created its small Mediation Support Unit of experts and augmented this with its Mediation Standby Team that has been deployed at short notice to backstop specific negotiations. Funding these efforts remains a perennial problem, however, and DPA remains under-resourced, given its expanding mandate. More specifically, the UN's capacity to support unanticipated missions remains a serious problem and relies principally on ad hoc donations from individual countries.

Besides these essentially political capacities, the UN can also authorize the deployment of military forces for preventive (as distinct from peacekeeping) missions. It has done so only once, however, with the UN Preventive Deployment Force to the former Yugoslav Republic of Macedonia from 1992 to 1999 to deter spillover from the conflicts in Bosnia and Kosovo. Though a useful precedent, a rare conjunction of circumstances—P5 unanimity, the acquiescence of a small host country, and the availability of UN forces nearby—made this possible. Whatever limited capacity the UN had to deploy forces quickly ended, moreover, with the termination of its Standby High-Readiness Brigade in 2009.

EUROPE

Among regional organizations, the capacity for preventive action varies widely. Europe, which has the EU, the OSCE, and NATO, possesses the most extensive—indeed redundant—set of multilateral capacities. Of the three, the OSCE has the most inclusive membership, with fifty-six states spanning a region "from Vancouver to Vladivostok." In addition to monitoring conventional force levels and activities among member states, the OSCE helps democratic institution building, promotes and safeguards minority rights, monitors elections, helps secure sensitive borders, and assists with security-sector reforms.

As an instrument for crisis prevention and crisis management, however, the OSCE has significant structural deficiencies that have hindered it from playing a significant role despite its declared intentions and array of diplomatic mechanisms.[16] In particular, the need for unanimity among member states has stymied rapid collective action on sensitive matters, as during the August 2008 crisis in Georgia, where Russia effectively blocked the OSCE from playing an active role, and in the delayed response to deadly ethnic riots in southern Kyrgyzstan in July 2010.[17] Recommendations amending the organization's decision-making rules to allow for greater initiative by senior officials in crisis circumstances were rejected at the most recent OSCE summit.[18]

Unlike the OSCE, the EU's conflict prevention role extends beyond its member states and has become one of the central goals of its externally directed Common Foreign and Security Policy (CFSP).[19] Since adopting the Program on the Prevention of Violent Conflict by the European Council in Göteborg in 2001, the EU has established a variety of special initiatives and institutional mechanisms for this purpose.[20] These range from foreign assistance programs intended to reduce the underlying risk of conflict through economic development and institution building in specific countries, particularly in Africa, to the Instrument for Stability, a short-term emergency assistance program for states in crisis.[21] The EU also maintains its own watchlist of countries at risk of violent conflict. Following the adoption of the European Security and Defense Policy (ESDP) in 2003, its capacity to deploy political and military missions for crisis management purposes has steadily grown.[22] To date there have been twenty-four crisis management operations, with thirteen ongoing as of June 2011.[23] These include police missions in Bosnia and Herzegovina, Kosovo, the Palestinian territories, and Afghanistan; rule of law missions in Kosovo and Iraq; and a monitoring mission in Georgia.[24] All are led by EU special representatives who can be "double-hatted" to oversee both military and diplomatic missions.

Reforms introduced by the 2009 Lisbon Treaty are designed, in theory, to improve the EU's crisis responsiveness and institutional flexibility.[25] The fragmented responses to the democratic uprisings in North Africa and the Middle East demonstrated, however, that member states will act faster and sometimes at odds with the consensus positions agreed to by the EU in Brussels. A new position, the high representative for foreign and security policy (who also serves as vice president of the commission), has been created, and parts of the commission and council secretariat have been amalgamated to form the European External Action Service. The Lisbon Treaty provides the high representative with considerable latitude to initiate foreign policy proposals, set the agenda of important EU bodies, including the Foreign Affairs Council (which he or she will chair), and convoke "extraordinary meetings [of the EU's council] on emergency matters."[26] The Lisbon Treaty establishes new procedures to provide "rapid access" to the EU budget and create a start-up fund of member state contributions outside the EU budget. Both procedures can finance "urgent initiatives" under the CFSP and, in particular, preparatory activities for ESDP missions. Decisions can be made by qualified majority voting, with the high representative authorized to disperse the funds.

In parallel with the development of a civilian expeditionary capability, the EU has also developed rapidly deployable military forces. Two "battle groups" are theoretically capable of deployment on five to ten days' notice for conflict prevention missions (preventive deployments, embargoes, counterproliferation, and joint disarmament operations).[27] To date, three wholly military ESDP missions have been deployed: Operation Artemis to the Democratic Republic of the Congo in 2003, Operation Concordia to Bosnia-Herzegovina in 2003, and EUFOR Chad/Central African Republic, which lasted from October 2007 until it was supplanted by a UN mission in March 2009.

LATIN AMERICA

The Organization of American States has made important strides toward playing a more active preventive role, even though its charter does not formally mandate it to do so. Its principal contributions to regional peace and stability relate to the promotion of democratic principles (through the Inter-American Democratic Charter and the Resolution 1080 mechanism that allows for violators to be condemned and isolated) and human rights (primarily through the Inter-American Commission on Human Rights that regularly issues reports of abuses).[28] Both activities exert a powerful normative influence throughout a region long blighted with coups and other extra-constitutional crises. Moreover, after being moribund for most of the Cold War, the OAS's various international dispute settlement mechanisms (principally the secretary-general's "good offices" and use of "special missions") have also successfully mediated territorial disputes involving Guatemala and Belize, Honduras and Nicaragua, and Guyana and Suriname.

OAS members, however, remain protective of the principle of non-intervention in internal disputes without host nation consent. Not surprisingly, therefore, OAS officials have been ambivalent to support norms like R2P and, at times, even the concept of *conflict prevention*, preferring instead the more consensual-sounding term *peacebuilding*. Its role in managing various ongoing internal conflicts in Latin America has consequently been relatively modest. Currently, the OAS has some analytical capabilities to warn of both internal instability and interstate disputes, but unless a member state appeals to the OAS Permanent Council and there is consensus to act, such warnings go unheeded.[29] Even when the will to act exists, the OAS's resources for mediation missions are limited.[30] Should peaceful preventive measures fail, the OAS has no deployable military or police forces within the region, though member states contribute to UN peacekeeping and special political missions. How the OAS evolves to fill some of these gaps will also depend on the development of a rival regional organization—the Union of South American Nations—that excludes the United States. Some members see this organization as becoming the premier political mechanism to resolve disputes, as demonstrated during the 2010 Colombian-Venezuelan crisis.

ASIA

The principal regional organization in Asia, the ASEAN, adheres to the same core principles as the OAS with regard to nonintervention and consensus-based decision-making. These principles are enshrined in the organization's Treaty of Amity and Cooperation and the 2008 ASEAN Charter, which commits signatories to settle their disputes peacefully, including refraining from threats to use force.[31] Unlike the OAS, however, ASEAN has done little to promote or uphold other normative principles conducive to stable peace, notably democratic governance and human rights. It has no electoral assistance or monitoring capabilities and few dispute resolution mechanisms or dedicated resources to facilitate mediation. The ASEAN Charter allows disputants to request the chair or secretary-general to act "in an ex officio capacity, to provide good offices, conciliation or mediation."[32] The current secretary-general has also tried to set a precedent by offering his services as a mediator, but so far he has been rebuffed. In particular, the secretary-general has made repeated, unsuccessful efforts in the past three years to resolve the Thai-Cambodian border dispute that erupted in June 2008. Plans to develop a rudimentary conflict early-warning system as part of an expanded operational role for the secretary-general and the ASEAN Secretariat may never happen.[33]

Elsewhere in Asia, the situation is even less developed. The South Asia Association for Regional Cooperation has no pretensions of playing a conflict prevention role other than by providing a regular venue for state leaders in the subcontinent to discuss their differences. The same is true for the Shanghai Cooperation Organization of central Asian states, though it is more security oriented in promoting cooperation on counterterrorism, border security, and even collective military action. As for Northeast Asia, no dedicated subregional organization exists, nor does one look likely anytime soon.[34]

THE MIDDLE EAST

Preventive efforts in the Middle East remain impoverished. Other than its rhetorical commitment to the peaceful resolution of disputes, some capacity for mediation, and a venue for dialogue among leaders in the Middle East, the Arab League plays virtually no significant role. Indeed, the league's well-known March 2011 resolution on Libya requested "that the UN Security Council fulfill its responsibilities," but made no requirements of its own member states to attempt to resolve the conflict in Libya.[35] The Gulf Cooperation Council (GCC) has historically been used only for functional collaboration that indirectly benefited regional stability.[36] However, in May 2011, the GCC made repeated, though ultimately unsuccessful, efforts to mediate an agreement between Yemeni president Ali Abdullah Saleh and opposition leaders, which would have granted Saleh immunity from prosecution had he left office within thirty days.

AFRICA

In Africa—the most conflict-prone region in the world—institutional development has improved markedly in recent years, although it falls short in important areas. In addition to the continent-wide AU, multiple subregional organizations—notably ECOWAS, the South Africa Development Community, the Inter-Governmental Authority on Development, and the Economic Community of Central African States—have all committed themselves to the goal of conflict prevention and initiated related programs. The African Union has increasingly emphasized norms that actively promote peace and stability in Africa. Whereas the AU's predecessor, the Organization of African Unity, was founded on principles of mutual noninterference amid African states newly independent of colonialism, the AU began a transition of non-indifference toward humanitarian disasters and violent conflict within the territory of member states.[37] Recognizing the ongoing scourge of armed violence, the AU assumed a leadership role in addressing conflicts in its own neighborhood. The Constitutive Act of the African Union expresses respect for borders and sovereignty and upholds "noninterference by any Member State in the internal affairs of another." It also affirms "the right of the Union to intervene in a Member State pursuant to a decision of the Assembly in respect of grave circumstances, namely war crimes, genocide and crimes against humanity" as well as "the right of Member States to request intervention from the Union in order to restore peace and security."[38]

The AU has also strongly endorsed the norm against unconstitutional political change in Africa, even permitting its Peace and Security Council the right to call on members to impose sanctions.[39] To date, the AU has called for sanctions three times. First, in May 2009, the AU sanctioned Eritrea for its assistance to Islamic militants fighting to overthrow the Transitional Federal Government in Somalia, which caused Eritrea to withdraw from the AU. Second, in October 2009, the AU sanctioned the military junta that took power in a coup in Guinea. Finally, the AU barred the Ivory Coast from participating in the organization from December 2010 until April 2011, during an internal power struggle when then president Laurent Gbagbo refused to step down after losing an election. Acting independently, or in conjunction with the AU, several African subregional organizations can also impose sanctions, with ECOWAS consistently being the most aggressive at doing so.

To buttress the AU's overall conflict prevention goals, various institutional capacities are being developed. The Continental Early Warning System was created in 2002 to report potential threats to the chairperson of the Commission of the AU, and in turn the organization's Peace and Security Council so that it can recommend timely action.[40] The leading subregional organizations have also begun developing conflict early-warning systems of varying degrees of effectiveness.[41] The AU has two primary dispute resolution mechanisms for conflict risk reduction and crisis mitigation. The first is the Panel of the Wise, consisting of five respected African personalities—one from each subregional organization—with a broad mandate to advise and support the Peace and Security Council and chairperson of the commission.[42] The panel has undertaken five fact-finding and mediations missions, including playing an active role in the successful mission in Kenya in 2008. The second are ad hoc high-level groups that have a poor track record with failed missions in Darfur in 2009 and Libya in 2011.

Finally, in 2003 the AU endorsed the concept of the African Standby Force to conduct a range of military missions, including "observation and monitoring . . . peace support . . . intervention in a Member State in respect of grave circumstances [and] preventive deployment," when mandated by the Peace and Security Council within the framework of the UN Charter.[43] The Standby Force aspires to include five multidisciplinary brigades—one provided by each African subregional organization—and be able to deploy anywhere on the continent within thirty days for peacekeeping missions, ninety days for complex peacekeeping operations, and fourteen days for interventions "in genocide situations where the international community does not act promptly."[44]

Although these considerable strides toward operationalizing preventive action in Africa should be lauded, their practical effect has been minimal. Even with the principle of non-indifference to political instability and violent conflict within member states enshrined in the AU's constitutive act, member states have not embraced R2P, a stance that will likely harden in light of the Libya intervention. Moreover, the AU's ability to implement its peace and security norms is hampered by the dynamics of the organization that operate by consensus. Some African leaders pay lip service to AU principles while actively blocking the more interventionist inclinations of others. Meanwhile, the new capacity-building initiatives are struggling to gain traction. The underresourced Panel of the Wise is often ignored by the commission or the Peace and Security Council. In light of its low profile and competing bodies—such as the AU high-level groups and the Nelson Mandela–convened Elders—there is deep concern within the AU that the panel will become irrelevant.[45]

Similarly, the AU's Military Staff Committee, which was established to manage and implement the goals set for the Standby Force, has made some initial steps in developing a common doctrine and guidelines for training and evaluation, but it has limited institutional capacity to do strategic planning, deploy soldiers, and conduct peacekeeping operations. Most important, the Standby Force requires outside funding as well as airlift and ground transport equipment for any crisis management situation.[46] Furthermore, the development of the five African subregional brigades is progressing at an uneven pace, with the ECOWAS Standby Force showing the most promise. Thus, the Standby Force failed to meet its goal of being operational by June 2010, and it now aims to have "rapid deployable capability" by 2012 and "full operational capability" by 2015.[47] Because the Standby Force cannot yet deploy as a unit, AU member states provide the vast majority of the twenty-three thousand peacekeepers and police officers supporting the joint AU/UN hybrid operation in Darfur and command the ten thousand African soldiers and police deployed in support of the AU Mission in Somalia.

Recommendations for U.S. Policy

Formal international institutions provide important benefits to the United States as it seeks to avoid the most serious risks associated with regional instability and conflict. The Obama administration has repeatedly underscored the imperatives of international cooperation and taken important steps to become a more active player in multilateral organizations, especially in the United Nations. However, if the United States is to harness the benefits of international cooperation for addressing its conflict prevention priorities, it must do so more strategically and systematically. In short, the United States must undertake a deliberate effort to enhance the global architecture for preventive action. *Architecture* in this sense refers to the institutions, regimes, operating procedures, and capacities of the numerous international organizations described above. The United States should pursue this goal in the three broad areas of preventive action—conflict risk reduction, crisis prevention, and conflict mitigation—recognizing that they can overlap and, more important, act in mutually reinforcing ways.

GLOBAL RISK REDUCTION INITIATIVES

The United States must continue to buttress the essential principles of world order enshrined in the UN Charter while supporting other emerging norms that regulate the use of force. The proscription of interstate aggression for territorial aggrandizement is universally accepted, but the parameters of permissible acts of anticipatory self-defense remain indistinct and may become more contested as states feel pressured to respond preemptively to emerging security threats that pose unacceptably high risks to the livelihoods of their citizens. Such pressures are already evident from several (overt and covert) counterproliferation and counterterrorism operations that have been carried out in recent years.

It is not hard to imagine how the imperatives to act against such threats will grow in the future with the global diffusion of deadly technologies, particularly to nonstate actors. Similar pressures to use force or intervene militarily could also conceivably grow in the face of other threats that stem from mass migration, the outbreak of deadly pandemics, and irresponsible environmental behavior. Defining precisely when anticipatory self-defense is permissible is beyond clear legal formulation; attempts to do so may have the unintended consequence of weakening existing charter-based rules. But just as the legality and legitimacy of humanitarian intervention has grown through the progressive endorsement of state behavior for this purpose, basic principles governing anticipatory self-defense—particularly as they relate to necessity and proportionality—may become acceptable in the future. Waiting for events to drive this process is risky, however, and thus the United States should quietly encourage debate in multilateral forums about how to reconcile the growing imperatives to act preemptively while maintaining the core foundations of international order.

Efforts to constrain the abuse of force by states within their territories has clearly advanced through miscellaneous international legal instruments that hold their leaders accountable and, more generally, through progressive UN actions in support of the R2P principle, including most overtly in Libya.[48] Many states—including powerful ones—are clearly uncomfortable with the invocation of R2P principles in light of its justification for coercive humanitarian intervention in Libya. The United States should endorse a narrower concept of R2P than was applied in Libya and put greater emphasis on earlier nonmilitary preventive action to avoid later, more costly military interventions that inevitably roil international relations among the great powers.[49] In support of this, the United States should provide voluntary contributions to enhance the analytical and response capacity of the joint special adviser for the prevention of genocide/R2P office, which has provided early and accurate warnings of sources of violent conflict. At the same time, the United States should consider joining the ICC and expand its diplomatic and informational support to it. In the near term, the Obama administration should push to overturn the 2001 law that prohibits providing material assistance to the ICC.[50]

Just as important as reducing the overall risk of conflict is promoting the normative basis of democracy, good governance, and economic freedom. The empirical evidence linking progress in these areas to peaceful relations between and within states is irrefutable. Robust multilateral institutions strengthen such norms through declarations and resolutions that provide legitimacy and encouragement to domestic civil society groups, as well as through the naming and shaming of transgressors that can become the basis for punitive action. Though the work of some international bodies, like the UN Human Rights Council, has at times been a sham, persistent engagement by the United States in relevant forums is preferable to walking away because it has allowed the United States to influence proceedings and improve matters from the inside. The UN's universal membership and corresponding broad legitimacy make it a particularly important instrument in the maintenance and evolution of desirable global norms. Yet the composition of the UN's governing core—the Security Council—no longer equitably reflects the distribution of power in the world today and will be increasingly viewed as illegitimate. The United States must work to reform the Security Council—both its membership and its operation rules—to ensure that it remains relevant and representative. Other global institutions that play a similar if more indirect role, such as the major IFIs, face a similar challenge. They too must be reformed or risk irrelevance.

Beyond efforts to strengthen normative principles, the United States should also endeavor to reinforce multilateral arrangements governing use of the so-called global commons—areas beyond sovereign jurisdiction such as the oceans, outer space, cyberspace, and the polar regions—where the risk of international competition is likely to grow in the coming decades as a result of climate change, technological advances that make these areas more accessible, and growing commercial pressures to exploit them.

GLOBAL CRISIS PREVENTION INITIATIVES

The United States should encourage and support the growing involvement of multilateral organizations in anticipating and forestalling sources of instability and conflict before they erupt. This approach has been evident in the work of the OECD's Development Assistance Committee, as well as within the leading IFIs as they increasingly make their guidance and assistance programming more sensitive to such dangers. The World Bank's 2011 World Development Report argues that this reorientation must go further and lays out a comprehensive set of recommendations for refocusing assistance to be more responsive in crisis situations.[51] Using its influence within the bank, the United States should support this and similar efforts at the IMF.

Closer U.S.-EU coordination of conflict prevention–related foreign assistance should also be pursued. The United States and the EU provide a huge proportion of OECD development aid yet do not adequately coordinate programs with respect to the specific goal of crisis prevention. The annual U.S.-EU summit is a logical opportunity to take collective stock of such short-term assistance needs that can then be pursued through the existing U.S. Agency for International Development (USAID) mission to the EU and the EU delegation to the United States. Similar initiatives to avoid duplication or working at cross-purposes should be pursued with donors at other multilateral organizations as well.[52]

Another objective should be to improve cooperation between the United States and the UN. First, the United States should help the UN and leading regional institutions carry out early warning and analysis of instability and potential armed conflicts. The United States has the most comprehensive intelligence collection and analysis system in the world. Using only open-source intelligence, the U.S. intelligence community should collaborate—in particular with the EU—in producing assessments of areas of potential instability to prioritize policymakers' near-term contingency planning. In addition, the State Department's Bureau of Intelligence and Research Humanitarian Information Unit should share its open-source conflict maps and socioeconomic reporting with early-warning units at the OSCE, AU, and OAS. Finally, despite calls for greater UN–regional organization cooperation, early-warning staffs at the UN and within these organizations note that there is no formal sharing of information, even for joint political or peacekeeping missions. Where possible, the United States should fund linkages in collecting information and sharing early-warning analyses.

On a diplomatic level, the United States should continue to increase its representation at major regional organizations, specifically in the AU and African regional economic communities. It was only in 2009 and 2011, respectively, that the State Department sent its first resident ambassadors to the AU and ASEAN. Only through presence within the secretariats of these organizations can the United States appreciate their concerns, influence day-to-day activities, and help shape work plans. It is also much easier to respond in a timely manner when more substantial diplomatic, humanitarian, and even military support is required.

Finally, and most important, the United States should increase its financial assistance to the UN and regional organizations for activities that help avert conflict. The United States already provides significant support to international organizations, funding 22 percent of the UN and 60 percent of the OAS regular budgets. Regular budgets, however, are hostage to maintaining the existing and underperforming infrastructure of most organizations. Small voluntary contributions, however, can support specific preventive programs—such as the $2 million that created the UN's special representative on sexual violence and conflict in 2010—and come with more rigorous oversight. Congress should provide voluntary funding on a competitive basis to international organizations through the State Department's international affairs budget. A competitive pool of $50 million to $100 million would have a direct and immediate impact on enhancing preventive capacity within each of the organizations described earlier. Metrics for assessing voluntary funding should include the absorptive capacity of the organization to effectively utilize it and the prioritization scheme also described. The competitive bidding system utilized by the independent and broadly popular Millennium Challenge Corporation is one model.

An obvious candidate for targeted voluntary contributions is the conflict prevention work of the Department of Political Affairs at the UN. Its request for greater funding between 2011 and 2013 is modest, but it could yield high returns for the United States.[53] Similar efforts to support electoral assistance programs at the UN and major regional organizations fall into the same category.

GLOBAL CONFLICT MITIGATION INITIATIVES

The United States can contribute to the international mitigation of conflict in two ways: by enhancing relevant organizations' capacity to respond promptly to crises and by providing timely operational support to these organizations during crises. With regard to the first category of initiatives, the United States should help the UN (principally DPA) and regional organizations improve their ability to augment field missions or mount new operations (fact-finding missions, commissions of inquiry, mediation support) at short notice. This can be achieved through targeted voluntary contributions of the kind out-lined earlier.

Although authorization for deployments of military and police forces during crises remains challenging, the Libyan intervention dem-onstrates that it remains a viable preventive option. Moreover, the pres-sure to use force preventively with international sanctions could grow as norms evolve. Rather than openly enhance the international capac-ity for such missions, which would meet international resistance, the United States should instead continue to augment more traditional peacekeeping capacity that by nature can be easily used in a preven-tive context. Various programs already exist to do this but more can be reoriented, particularly toward training and equipping.[54] Just by releas-ing nonlethal Pentagon stockpiles, the United States could fill critical equipment needs for armored personnel carriers, utility helicopters, and aerial reconnaissance, which have been missing from the UN/AU mission in Darfur for five years. Again, greater cooperation with the EU and NATO on this issue should be pursued.

With regard to the second category of assistance, the United States should enhance its readiness to contribute support in emergency situ-ations. Congress should authorize the Obama administration's pro-posed $50 million Global Security Contingency Fund, which would be operated by a joint State Department, USAID, and Department of Defense staff, to disburse rapid security assistance funding in the face of unforeseen emergent challenges. The U.S. intelligence community should also increase the intelligence it shares with the UN regarding threats to deployed peacekeepers and staff. UN Department of Peace-keeping Operations (DPKO) officials have noted that such threat intel-ligence was "too late, too vague, and too ad-hoc" for adequate warning. There needs to be an institutionalized U.S.-DPKO mechanism for sharing more descriptive intelligence at an earlier stage. One possibility is for the director of national intelligence to designate a U.S. military official, who is presently seconded to serve at the UN, as the conduit for intelligence sharing with DPKO.[55]

Conclusion

These various recommendations to enhance the architecture of formal international institutions for preventive action represent an ambitious agenda. As such, they cannot possibly be accomplished quickly. A sustained commitment will therefore be necessary to achieve the anticipated benefits. This will not be easy, given the prevailing doubts about the role of many international organizations that will likely grow more acute as Washington looks to tighten its belt. Overcoming this skepticism will require continued advocacy at the highest levels of the U.S. government. It will also require similar commitments from other leading players in the international community in order to avoid perceptions that the United States bears this burden alone. While difficult, it is important that the Obama administration and Congress adopt these recommendations to avoid further commitment of military forces, financial and humanitarian aid, and diplomatic attention to violent conflict and instability in regions that directly affect U.S. interests but are rarely effectively resolved.

Endnotes

1. Paul B. Stares and Micah Zenko, *Enhancing U.S. Preventive Action* (New York: Council on Foreign Relations Press, 2009).
2. For definitions of these three categories, see *Enhancing U.S. Preventive Action*, pp. 7–8.
3. Ian Johnstone, "Normative Evolution at the UN: Impact of Operational Activities," in Bruce D. Jones, Shepherd Forman, and Richard Gowan, eds., *Cooperating for Peace and Security: Evolving Institutions and Arrangement in the Context of Changing U.S. Security Policy* (New York: Cambridge University Press, 2010), p. 202.
4. For an assessment of the R2P norm see Matthew C. Waxman, *Intervention to Stop Genocide and Mass Atrocities* (New York: Council on Foreign Relations Press, 2009), pp. 10–11.
5. Johnstone, "Normative Evolution at the UN: Impact of Operational Activities," pp. 193–95.
6. See Congressional Research Service Memorandum to Senate Foreign Relations Committee, "Peacebuilding Background and Questions," May 27, 2010, p. 11.
7. See United Nations Development Program (UNDP), *Elections and Conflict Prevention: A Guide to Analysis, Planning and Programming*, http://www.undp.org/publications/Elections_and_Conflict_Prevention.pdf.
8. Interviews with UN Department of Political Affairs/UNDP officials.
9. Michèle Griffin, "Rapid Political Response: A View from Turtle Bay," working paper, Stanley Foundation Strategy for Peace Conference, October 15–17, 2009.
10. For an assessment of UN early-warning capacities, see Micah Zenko and Rebecca R. Friedman, "UN Early Warning for Preventing Conflict," *International Peacekeeping*, vol. 18, no. 1, February 2011.
11. UNGA, "Report of the Secretary-General: Early warning, assessment and the responsibility to protect," July 14, 2010, p. 4. The UN also established a special adviser for the prevention of genocide with responsibilities to warn the public of impending mass atrocities and "convene an urgent meeting of key undersecretaries-general to identify a range of multilateral policy options."
12. See UNGA, "Prevention of armed conflict: Report of the Secretary-General," June 7, 2001.
13. UN Department of Political Affairs, "Policy Coordination: The Executive Committee on Peace and Security"; Rama Mani, "Peaceful Settlement of Disputes and Conflict Prevention," in Thomas G. Weiss and Sam Daws, eds., *The Oxford Handbook* (Oxford: Oxford University Press, 2007), p. 315; UN, "In Larger Freedom: Towards Development, Security and Human Rights for All," Report of the Secretary-General, March 21, 2005, p. 47.
14. The Framework Team consists of representatives from twenty-two agencies and departments—though only five or six are active participants. It meets in plenary three or four times a year and convenes expert reference group meetings twice a month to discuss countries or thematic issues.

15. See Theresa Whitfield, "New Arrangements for Peace Negotiation," in Bruce D. Jones, Shepard Forman, and Richard Gowan, eds., *Cooperating for Peace and Security* (New York: Cambridge University Press, 2010), pp. 227–46.

16. The OSCE has no institutionalized conflict risk assessment/watch list system because it has no mandate to monitor events either within or beyond the territorial limits of its member states. The seven-person OSCE Situation/Communications Room in the Conflict Prevention Center in Vienna produces a twice-daily compilation of open-source reports and internal communications from OSCE field missions for senior officials. These are also shared with the EU and NATO SITCENs under a reciprocal arrangement. The Situation/Communications Room has also developed an SMS-based system to warn senior officials of breaking news. Similarly, the OSCE has no authority to carry out contingency planning for potential missions. The OSCE has institutional mechanisms to respond to emergency conflict-related situations and resolve them peacefully, including the Berlin Mechanism, whereby states are obliged to provide information within forty-eight hours following a request from another member for clarification of an evolving situation; the Valletta Mechanism, which lays out procedures for the peaceful resolution of disputes; and the OSCE Convention on Conciliation and Arbitration. Only the Berlin Mechanism has been implemented. OSCE Secretariat, "Summary of OSCE Mechanisms and Procedures," June 2008.

17. In response to rising tensions in Georgia, a group of OSCE ambassadors were dispatched to Georgia in July on a fact-finding mission. Once hostilities erupted, the chairman-in-office (the OSCE's most senior permanent official) engaged in personal shuttle diplomacy in the region and an additional twenty military monitoring officers (out of eighty authorized) were sent within days to bolster the OSCE mission in Georgia. Russia, however, vetoed continuation of the mission in December 2008. See "Statement by OSCE Secretary General Marc Perrin De Brichambaut at the Sixteenth OSCE Ministerial Council meeting," Helsinki, December 4, 2008.

18. See "After the Astana Summit: More Questions than Answers," Policy Brief No. 9, Center for Strategic and International Studies and Institute for New Democracies, December 17, 2010.

19. Reinhardt Rummel, "The EU's Involvement in Conflict Prevention—Strategy and Practice," in Jan Wouters and Vincent Kronnenberger, eds., *Conflict Prevention: Is the European Union Ready?* (Brussels: TMC Asser Press, 2004); and Emma J. Stewart, *The European Union and Conflict Prevention*, Kiel Peace Research Series, vol. 12, 2006.

20. EU Programme on the Prevention of Violent Conflict, 2001. This states that the European Union "through this programme underlines its political commitment to pursue conflict prevention as one of the main objectives of the EU's external relations." It distinguishes between long-term "structural prevention" to reduce the risk of instability and conflict in weak and fragile states—principally through foreign assistance programs—and "short-term" preventive diplomacy to manage crises and halt the outbreak of conflict. The EU's 2008 annual report on its conflict prevention activities further distinguishes "systemic prevention" measures to reduce the risk of instability through global regulatory regimes affecting, among other things, the exploitation of natural resources, climate change, organized crime, weapons of mass destruction (WMD) proliferation, and the transfer of small arms and light weapons.

21. European Commission, *Annual Report from the European Commission on the Instrument for Stability in 2009*, September 28, 2010. The amount of funds disbursed for crisis response as part of the IfS budget has increased from €93 million in 2007 to €132 million in 2009. The IfS also has a long-term component focused primarily on countering WMD, proliferation, terrorism, and a "pre-crisis and post-crisis capacity-building" component.

22. The watch list is created using a combination of quantitative and qualitative method-
    ologies with inputs from DG-Relex as well as the EU's Joint Situation Center, which
    monitors day-to-day events around the world, and the Intelligence Division of the EU's
    Military Staff (EUMS), which is tasked with assessing "current and emerging areas of
    instability." Information for the watch list and other related assessments comes from
    multiple sources: intelligence inputs from member states, reports for EU delegations,
    EU special representatives in the field, and also the European Satellite Center. As a
    result of partnership agreements, the EU also exchanges information with the UN and
    OSCE and other international bodies. NATO, however, reportedly contributes little
    of value to the EU SITCEN, which is the source of some frustration. Major General
    João Nuno Jorge Vaz Antunes, "Developing an Intelligence Capability," *Studies in Intel-
    ligence,* vol. 49, no. 4, 2005, pp. 65–70.

23. EU Common Security and Defence Policy, "Overview of the Mission and Operations
    of the European Union, March 2011," http://www.consilium.europa.eu/eeas/security-
    defence/eu-operations.aspx?lang=en.

24. For more details, see European Common Security and Defence Policy, "The Civilian
    Aspects of Crisis Management," EU Council Secretariat, August 2009.

25. "Treaty of Lisbon amending the Treaty on European Union and the Treaty establishing
    the European Community," Lisbon, December 13, 2007.

26. See "A More Coherent and Effective European Foreign Policy?" *A Report of the UK
    Federal Trust for Education and Research,* February 2009, pp. 12–13.

27. Since adopting the "Petersberg Tasks" in 1992, the EU has expanded the spectrum of
    missions it has collectively committed to perform using military means if necessary.
    The Lisbon Treaty further refines these tasks to include "joint disarmament operations
    . . . military advice and assistance tasks . . . conflict prevention and peace-keeping tasks
    . . . peace-making and post-conflict stabilisation" and also to contribute to combating
    terrorism "by supporting third countries . . . in their territories" (article 28B, paragraph
    1). Responsibility for maintaining these national and multinational constituted battle
    groups are rotated every six months within the EU. See EU Factsheet at http://www.
    consilium.europa.eu/uedocs/cmsUpload/Battlegroups.pdf.

28. OAS, *IACHR Annual Report 2008,* "Chapter III: The Petition and Case System,"
    2009. The IACHR also maintains eight rapporteurs for thematic issues, who publish
    warnings of violations within OAS member states. In addition, the commission can
    refer cases to the autonomous Inter-American Court of Human Rights, which has
    issued far-reaching provisional measures for action by member states, including in
    "cases of extreme gravity and urgency." See OAS, American Convention, Article 63(2).

29. The OAS has two early-warning and assessment units within its Secretariat of Political
    Affairs' Department of Sustainable Democracy and Special Missions (DSDME).
    Developed in 2006, the first provides intrastate warning for countries at risk of
    political crisis. A small unit of analysts collects information and produces reports
    based on twenty political, social, and economic indicators, or "accelerators," for each
    country. In addition to collecting data on these indicators, the unit holds informal
    "Delphi groups," or focus groups, in countries of concern with academics, corporate
    executives, and members of the media and civil society. The main intrastate warning
    products created are weekly and monthly reports, as well as biannual country-specific
    reports. A second and separate early-warning unit within DSDME covers potential
    interstate conflicts. Reporting from both units is shared only with the director for
    DSDME, the Secretariat of Political Affairs, and the secretary-general. Warnings of
    potential intrastate or interstate conflicts do not trigger contingency planning or other
    specific preventive activities. Interviews with OAS staff; and Andres Serbin, "The
    Organization of American States, the United Nations Organization, Civil Society,

and Conflict Prevention," Coordinadora Regional de Investigaciones Económicas y Sociales, March 2009. There is a mandated dispute resolution mechanism used during crises through the Meeting of Consultation of Ministers of Foreign Affairs, held "in order to consider problems of an urgent nature and of common interest to the member states of the Organization of American States." See "Meetings of the Consultation of Ministers of Foreign Affairs," http://www.oas.org/en/about/meetings_foreign_affairs.asp. According to OAS officials, this has proven too slow and ineffective for the most pressing issues, as foreign ministers can only convene after a member state has appealed to the Permanent Council and the council votes to permit a meeting.

30. In practice, the secretary-general selects special representatives on a periodic basis for OAS mediation efforts, either independently or when mandated by the Permanent Council. The Secretariat maintains no formal roster of former diplomats or government officials to call upon, and there is no dedicated mediation support capacity to support OAS-mandated mediation. Senior officials, and country or thematic experts from the Secretariat for Political Affairs, however, are routinely called upon to provide technical and political support to OAS mediation efforts or special missions. Interviews with OAS staff; Serbin, "The Organization of American States, the United Nations Organization, Civil Society, and Conflict Prevention," pp. 7–12.

31. Over the past five years, ASEAN has entered into a number of agreements that promote greater integration and transparency in areas such as economic development, energy security, and education. In November 2007, at the Thirteenth ASEAN Summit, the heads of state put forth the long-term goal of creating an ASEAN Community by 2015 to consist of three components: the ASEAN Economic Community, which aims to promote economic integration through internal free trade; the ASEAN Political Security Community, which aspires to "promote political development in adherence to the principles of democracy, the rule of law and good governance, respect for and promotion and protection of human rights and fundamental freedoms as inscribed in the ASEAN Charter"; and the ASEAN Socio-Cultural Community, whose primary goal "is to contribute to realizing an ASEAN Community that is people-centered and socially responsible with a view to achieving enduring solidarity and unity among the nations and peoples of ASEAN." In 2009, the Secretariat published a framework and work plan for achieving an ASEAN Community by 2015. ASEAN, *Roadmap for an ASEAN Community: 2009–2015*, 2009.

32. ASEAN, *The ASEAN Charter*, Article 23, adopted by all member states in 2008.

33. Interviews with UN staff and regional experts. For plans to create an early warning system, see ASEAN, *ASEAN Political-Security Blueprint*, June 2009, p. 9.

34. For a useful essay on the problems and prospects for multilateralism in Asia, see Evan A. Feigenbaum and Robert A. Manning, *The United States in the New Asia*, Council Special Report No. 50 (New York: Council on Foreign Relations Press, 2009).

35. Council of the League of Arab States, "Repercussions of Current Events in Libya and the Arab Position Thereupon," March 12, 2011.

36. For a comprehensive assessment of the role of the Arab League and GCC for conflict mediation see Marco Pinfari, "Nothing But Failure? The Arab League and the Gulf Cooperation Council as Mediators in Middle Eastern Conflict," Crisis States Research Centre Working Paper No. 45, London School of Economics, March 2009.

37. AU, "Foreword," *Meeting the Challenge of Conflict Prevention in Africa: Towards the Operationalization of the Continental Early Warning System*, 2008, p. 2.

38. AU, "Constitutive Act of the African Union," Article 4, July 11, 2000.

39. Ibid., Article 23; AU, "Protocol Relating to the Establishment of the Peace and Security Council of the African Union," Article 7(g), July 9, 2002.

40. AU, "Protocol Related to the Establishment of the Peace and Security Council of the African Union," Article 12, July 9, 2002. The CEWS aims to consist of two

components. The first is the twenty-four-hour Situation Room located within the Peace and Security Directorate's Conflict Management Division in Addis Ababa. The Situation Room has a staff of thirteen and serves as the point of contact between the commission and member states, African Regional Economic Communities (RECs), and NGOs. It also collects data from open sources, AU field missions, and RECs for indicators of potential or ongoing conflicts, which is then screened and disseminated to analysts within the Peace and Security Council. See European Union delegation to the AU, "Inside the African Union Situation Room," October 2009, pp. 16–17.

41. The most developed is the ECOWAS's Early Warning and Response Network (ECOWARN). Situated in the Office of the Commissioner for Political Affairs, Peace and Security, ECOWARN consists of four subregional zonal bureaus—located in Benin, Burkina Faso, Liberia, and Gambia—that collect and evaluate data based on ninety-four conflict indicators, primarily from open sources and NGOs but also from some member states, and an Observation and Monitoring Centre at the ECOWAS Commission in Abuja that produces analytical warning reports. See "The ECOWAS Conflict Prevention Framework," January 1, 2008; and Organization for Economic Cooperation and Development, *SWAC News*, April-May 2009, pp. 2–4. IGAD operates an early-warning system in Ethiopia, Kenya, and Uganda—the Committee on Early Warning and Response—focused primarily on pastoralist conflicts. ECCAS operates the Early Warning Mechanism of Central Africa. The framework for harmonizing the early-warning units of the subregional organizations with the AU's CEWS failed to become fully operational by its goal of 2009. See AU, "Framework for the Operationalization of the Continental Early Warning System as Adopted by the Governmental Experts Meeting on Early Warning and Prevention," December 17–19, 2006.

42. AU, "Protocol Related to the Establishment of the Peace and Security Council of the African Union," Article 11, July 9, 2002.

43. Ibid., Article 13.

44. AU, "Policy Framework for the Establishment of the African Standby Force and the Military Staff Committee," adopted by the Third Meeting of the African Chiefs of Defense Staff, May 15–16, 2003; AU, Experts' Meeting on the Relationship Between the AU and the Regional Mechanisms for Conflict Prevention, Management, and Resolution, "Roadmap for the Operationalization of the African Standby Force," March 22–23, 2005.

45. Interviews with UN staff and regional experts; El Abdellaoui, "The Panel of the Wise: A Comprehensive Introduction to a Critical Pillar of the African Peace and Security Architecture," ISS Paper No. 193, Institute for Security Studies, August 2009, p. 8; AU, "Seventh Meeting of the Panel of the Wise," November 19, 2009.

46. Interview with State Department staff, January 2010. State has funded a logistics depot with some transportation equipment at ECOWAS.

47. Interviews with UN staff and regional experts; AU, "Progress Report on the Status of the Operationalization of the African Standby Force," December 3–7, 2010, p. 1.

48. Although President Obama never explicitly linked the NATO-led military intervention in Libya in March 2011 with R2P, cabinet members and foreign political leaders acknowledged that it was the first time the norm was implemented with military force. However, the expansion of NATO's initial military objectives—enforcing a no-fly zone, enforcing an arms embargo, and protecting civilian populations—to include providing close air support for the armed rebels and targeting Muammar al-Qaddafi, has eroded support for R2P among some emerging powers. In light of the Libya intervention, a draft Security Council resolution condemning the Syrian government for attacks on its civilian populations was rejected by Russia and China. Russian president Dmitry Medvedev noted that the Libya resolution was "turned into a scrap

of paper to cover up a pointless military operation. . . . I would very much not like a Syrian resolution to be pulled off in a similar manner. See Charles Clover, "Medvedev Stance Dims Hope for UN Syria Vote," *Financial Times*, June 19, 2011. In addition, AU heads of state in early July declared that with regards to an ICC arrest warrant of Qaddafi, "the Assembly decided that AU Member States shall not cooperate in the execution of the arrest warrant." See AU, "Decisions Adopted During the 17th African Union Summit," July 1, 2011.

49. See Waxman, *Intervention to Stop Genocide and Mass Atrocities*.

50. A January 2010 Department of Justice memorandum concluded that diplomatic or informational support for "particular investigations or prosecutions" by the ICC does not violate U.S. laws. However, the effect of the 2001 law means that there is not timely and reliable cooperation between the State Department and Pentagon and ICC Headquarters in The Hague. Congressional Research Service, "International Criminal Court Cases in Africa: Status and Policy Issues," March 7, 2011, p. 4.

51. See World Bank, *World Development Report 2011: Conflict, Security and Development*, April 2011.

52. The capacity-building programs for regional organizations by the United States are not coordinated with those led by other countries, organizations, or NGOs. State Department and USAID officials noted that there was insufficient understanding between the United States and EU on who was focused on what issue in regards to supporting the African Union. The same lack of coordination is true for ASEAN, where there is a monthly meeting at the Secretariat in Jakarta, but some countries either do not participate (China) or merely inform each other of ongoing projects. In addition, regional organizations are content with receiving whatever funding or assistance that can be provided, and so on their own will not mandate coordination between donors. To better assure that well-meaning states, organizations, and NGOs are not working at cross-purposes, the United States should take a lead role in producing prioritized and coordinated work plans for all prospective donors.

53. See UN Department of Political Affairs, *DPA Multi-Year Appeal 2011–2013*, November 2010.

54. For a list of useful initiatives, see Ron Capps, *In Our Stead: Developing and Enhancing International Security Assistance Capacities*, the Stanley Foundation, 2009.

55. For equipment shortages in Darfur, see UN, "Report of the Secretary-General on the African Union-United Nations Hybrid in Darfur (UNAMID)," April 14, 2011, p. 12.

About the Authors

Paul B. Stares is the General John W. Vessey senior fellow for conflict prevention and director of the Center for Preventive Action (CPA) at the Council on Foreign Relations (CFR). Prior to joining CFR, Stares was the vice president and director of the Center for Conflict Analysis and Prevention at the United States Institute of Peace. He worked as an associate director and senior research scholar at Stanford University's Center for International Security and Cooperation from 2000 to 2002 and was a senior research fellow at the Japan Institute of International Affairs and then director of studies at the Japan Center for International Exchange from 1996 to 2000. From 1984 to 1996, he was a research associate and later a senior fellow in the foreign policy studies program at the Brookings Institution. He has also been a NATO fellow and a scholar-in-residence at the MacArthur Foundation's Moscow office. He is the author or editor of ten books and numerous articles and reports, including most recently the CFR publications "Enhancing U.S Crisis Preparedness" (Policy Innovation Memorandum No. 4), "Military Escalation in Korea" (Contingency Planning Memorandum No. 10), *Enhancing U.S. Preventive Action* (Council Special Report No. 48), and *Preparing for Sudden Change in North Korea* (Council Special Report No. 42).

Micah Zenko is a fellow for conflict prevention in the Center for Preventive Action at the Council on Foreign Relations. Previously, he worked for five years at Harvard University's Kennedy School of Government in a number of research positions, and in Washington, DC, at the Brookings Institution, the Congressional Research Service, and the State Department's Office of Policy Planning. Zenko has published on a range of national security issues, including articles in the *Journal of Strategic Studies, Parameters, Defense and Security Analysis*, and *Annals of the American Academy of Political and Social Science*, and op-eds in the

Washington Post, Los Angeles Times, Chicago Tribune, Boston Globe, Foreign Policy, and the websites of the *New York Times* and *Foreign Affairs.* He writes the blog "Politics, Power, and Preventive Action" on CFR.org, which covers U.S. national security policy, international security, and conflict prevention. He is the author of two Council Special Reports, *Enhancing U.S. Preventive Action,* with CPA director Paul Stares, and *Toward Deeper Reductions in U.S. and Russian Nuclear Weapons.* Dr. Zenko received a PhD in political science from Brandeis University. His book, *Between Threats and War: U.S. Discrete Military Operations in the Post–Cold War World,* was published by Stanford University Press in September 2010.

Advisory Committee for
Partners in Preventive Action

Adonia Ayebare
*Permanent Mission of the Republic
of Uganda to the UN*

John Campbell, *ex officio*
Council on Foreign Relations

Michèle Griffin
United Nations

David Haeri
United Nations

Matthew L. Hodes

Jolyon Howorth
Yale University

Bruce Jones
New York University

Jacques Paul Klein
United Nations

Chetan Kumar
United Nations Development Programme

Kara C. McDonald, *ex officio*
Council on Foreign Relations

Joyce Neu
The Carter Center

Steven M. Siqueira

James B. Sitrick
Baker & McKenzie LLP

Nancy E. Soderberg
University of North Florida

Yadira Soto
Organization of American States

Frederick S. Tipson
United Nations Development Programme

James Traub
New York Times Magazine

Joanna Weschler
Security Council Report

Richard S. Williamson
Chicago Council on Global Affairs

Lawrence S. Woocher

CPA Advisory Committee

Mission Statement of the Center for Preventive Action

The Center for Preventive Action (CPA) seeks to help prevent, defuse, or resolve deadly conflicts around the world and to expand the body of knowledge on conflict prevention. It does so by creating a forum in which representatives of governments, international organizations, nongovernmental organizations, corporations, and civil society can gather to develop operational and timely strategies for promoting peace in specific conflict situations. The center focuses on conflicts in countries or regions that affect U.S. interests, but may be otherwise overlooked; where prevention appears possible; and when the resources of the Council on Foreign Relations can make a difference. The center does this by

- Issuing Council Special Reports to evaluate and respond rapidly to developing conflict situations and formulate timely, concrete policy recommendations that the U.S. government, international community, and local actors can use to limit the potential for deadly violence.
- Engaging the U.S. government and news media in conflict prevention efforts. CPA staff members meet with administration officials and members of Congress to brief on CPA's findings and recommendations; facilitate contacts between U.S. officials and important local and external actors; and raise awareness among journalists of potential flashpoints around the globe.
- Building networks with international organizations and institutions to complement and leverage the Council's established influence in the U.S. policy arena and increase the impact of CPA's recommendations.
- Providing a source of expertise on conflict prevention to include research, case studies, and lessons learned from past conflicts that policymakers and private citizens can use to prevent or mitigate future deadly conflicts.

Council Special Reports

Published by the Council on Foreign Relations

Justice Beyond The Hague: Supporting the Prosecution of International Crimes in National Courts
David A. Kaye; CSR No. 61, June 2011

The Drug War in Mexico: Confronting a Shared Threat
David A. Shirk; CSR No. 60, March 2011
A Center for Preventive Action Report

UN Security Council Enlargement and U.S. Interests
Kara C. McDonald and Stewart M. Patrick; CSR No. 59, December 2010
An International Institutions and Global Governance Program Report

Congress and National Security
Kay King; CSR No. 58, November 2010

Toward Deeper Reductions in U.S. and Russian Nuclear Weapons
Micah Zenko; CSR No. 57, November 2010
A Center for Preventive Action Report

Internet Governance in an Age of Cyber Insecurity
Robert K. Knake; CSR 56, September 2010
An International Institutions and Global Governance Program Report

From Rome to Kampala: The U.S. Approach to the 2010 International Criminal Court Review Conference
Vijay Padmanabhan; CSR No. 55, April 2010

Strengthening the Nuclear Nonproliferation Regime
Paul Lettow; CSR No. 54, April 2010
An International Institutions and Global Governance Program Report

The Russian Economic Crisis
Jeffrey Mankoff; CSR No. 53, April 2010

Somalia: A New Approach
Bronwyn E. Bruton; CSR No. 52, March 2010
A Center for Preventive Action Report

The Future of NATO
James M. Goldgeier; CSR No. 51, February 2010
An International Institutions and Global Governance Program Report

The United States in the New Asia
Evan A. Feigenbaum and Robert A. Manning; CSR No. 50, November 2009
An International Institutions and Global Governance Program Report

Intervention to Stop Genocide and Mass Atrocities: International Norms and U.S. Policy
Matthew C. Waxman; CSR No. 49, October 2009
An International Institutions and Global Governance Program Report

Enhancing U.S. Preventive Action
Paul B. Stares and Micah Zenko; CSR No. 48, October 2009
A Center for Preventive Action Report

The Canadian Oil Sands: Energy Security vs. Climate Change
Michael A. Levi; CSR No. 47, May 2009
A Maurice R. Greenberg Center for Geoeconomic Studies Report

The National Interest and the Law of the Sea
Scott G. Borgerson; CSR No. 46, May 2009

Lessons of the Financial Crisis
Benn Steil; CSR No. 45, March 2009
A Maurice R. Greenberg Center for Geoeconomic Studies Report

Global Imbalances and the Financial Crisis
Steven Dunaway; CSR No. 44, March 2009
A Maurice R. Greenberg Center for Geoeconomic Studies Report

Eurasian Energy Security
Jeffrey Mankoff; CSR No. 43, February 2009

Preparing for Sudden Change in North Korea
Paul B. Stares and Joel S. Wit; CSR No. 42, January 2009
A Center for Preventive Action Report

Averting Crisis in Ukraine
Steven Pifer; CSR No. 41, January 2009
A Center for Preventive Action Report

Congo: Securing Peace, Sustaining Progress
Anthony W. Gambino; CSR No. 40, October 2008
A Center for Preventive Action Report

Deterring State Sponsorship of Nuclear Terrorism
Michael A. Levi; CSR No. 39, September 2008

China, Space Weapons, and U.S. Security
Bruce W. MacDonald; CSR No. 38, September 2008

Sovereign Wealth and Sovereign Power: The Strategic Consequences of American Indebtedness
Brad W. Setser; CSR No. 37, September 2008
A Maurice R. Greenberg Center for Geoeconomic Studies Report

Securing Pakistan's Tribal Belt
Daniel Markey; CSR No. 36, July 2008 (Web-only release) and August 2008
A Center for Preventive Action Report

Avoiding Transfers to Torture
Ashley S. Deeks; CSR No. 35, June 2008

Global FDI Policy: Correcting a Protectionist Drift
David M. Marchick and Matthew J. Slaughter; CSR No. 34, June 2008
A Maurice R. Greenberg Center for Geoeconomic Studies Report

Dealing with Damascus: Seeking a Greater Return on U.S.-Syria Relations
Mona Yacoubian and Scott Lasensky; CSR No. 33, June 2008
A Center for Preventive Action Report

Climate Change and National Security: An Agenda for Action
Joshua W. Busby; CSR No. 32, November 2007
A Maurice R. Greenberg Center for Geoeconomic Studies Report

Planning for Post-Mugabe Zimbabwe
Michelle D. Gavin; CSR No. 31, October 2007
A Center for Preventive Action Report

The Case for Wage Insurance
Robert J. LaLonde; CSR No. 30, September 2007
A Maurice R. Greenberg Center for Geoeconomic Studies Report

Reform of the International Monetary Fund
Peter B. Kenen; CSR No. 29, May 2007
A Maurice R. Greenberg Center for Geoeconomic Studies Report

Nuclear Energy: Balancing Benefits and Risks
Charles D. Ferguson; CSR No. 28, April 2007

Nigeria: Elections and Continuing Challenges
Robert I. Rotberg; CSR No. 27, April 2007
A Center for Preventive Action Report

The Economic Logic of Illegal Immigration
Gordon H. Hanson; CSR No. 26, April 2007
A Maurice R. Greenberg Center for Geoeconomic Studies Report

The United States and the WTO Dispute Settlement System
Robert Z. Lawrence; CSR No. 25, March 2007
A Maurice R. Greenberg Center for Geoeconomic Studies Report

Bolivia on the Brink
Eduardo A. Gamarra; CSR No. 24, February 2007
A Center for Preventive Action Report

After the Surge: The Case for U.S. Military Disengagement from Iraq
Steven N. Simon; CSR No. 23, February 2007

Darfur and Beyond: What Is Needed to Prevent Mass Atrocities
Lee Feinstein; CSR No. 22, January 2007

Avoiding Conflict in the Horn of Africa: U.S. Policy Toward Ethiopia and Eritrea
Terrence Lyons; CSR No. 21, December 2006
A Center for Preventive Action Report

Living with Hugo: U.S. Policy Toward Hugo Chávez's Venezuela
Richard Lapper; CSR No. 20, November 2006
A Center for Preventive Action Report

Reforming U.S. Patent Policy: Getting the Incentives Right
Keith E. Maskus; CSR No. 19, November 2006
A Maurice R. Greenberg Center for Geoeconomic Studies Report

Foreign Investment and National Security: Getting the Balance Right
Alan P. Larson and David M. Marchick; CSR No. 18, July 2006
A Maurice R. Greenberg Center for Geoeconomic Studies Report

Challenges for a Postelection Mexico: Issues for U.S. Policy
Pamela K. Starr; CSR No. 17, June 2006 (Web-only release) and November 2006

U.S.-India Nuclear Cooperation: A Strategy for Moving Forward
Michael A. Levi and Charles D. Ferguson; CSR No. 16, June 2006

Generating Momentum for a New Era in U.S.-Turkey Relations
Steven A. Cook and Elizabeth Sherwood-Randall; CSR No. 15, June 2006

Peace in Papua: Widening a Window of Opportunity
Blair A. King; CSR No. 14, March 2006
A Center for Preventive Action Report

Neglected Defense: Mobilizing the Private Sector to Support Homeland Security
Stephen E. Flynn and Daniel B. Prieto; CSR No. 13, March 2006

Afghanistan's Uncertain Transition From Turmoil to Normalcy
Barnett R. Rubin; CSR No. 12, March 2006
A Center for Preventive Action Report

Preventing Catastrophic Nuclear Terrorism
Charles D. Ferguson; CSR No. 11, March 2006

Getting Serious About the Twin Deficits
Menzie D. Chinn; CSR No. 10, September 2005
A Maurice R. Greenberg Center for Geoeconomic Studies Report

Both Sides of the Aisle: A Call for Bipartisan Foreign Policy
Nancy E. Roman; CSR No. 9, September 2005

Forgotten Intervention? What the United States Needs to Do in the Western Balkans
Amelia Branczik and William L. Nash; CSR No. 8, June 2005
A Center for Preventive Action Report

A New Beginning: Strategies for a More Fruitful Dialogue with the Muslim World
Craig Charney and Nicole Yakatan; CSR No. 7, May 2005

Power-Sharing in Iraq
David L. Phillips; CSR No. 6, April 2005
A Center for Preventive Action Report

Giving Meaning to "Never Again": Seeking an Effective Response to the Crisis in Darfur and Beyond
Cheryl O. Igiri and Princeton N. Lyman; CSR No. 5, September 2004

Freedom, Prosperity, and Security: The G8 Partnership with Africa: Sea Island 2004 and Beyond
J. Brian Atwood, Robert S. Browne, and Princeton N. Lyman; CSR No. 4, May 2004

Addressing the HIV/AIDS Pandemic: A U.S. Global AIDS Strategy for the Long Term
Daniel M. Fox and Princeton N. Lyman; CSR No. 3, May 2004
Cosponsored with the Milbank Memorial Fund

Challenges for a Post-Election Philippines
Catharin E. Dalpino; CSR No. 2, May 2004
A Center for Preventive Action Report

Stability, Security, and Sovereignty in the Republic of Georgia
David L. Phillips; CSR No. 1, January 2004
A Center for Preventive Action Report

To purchase a printed copy, call the Brookings Institution Press: 800.537.5487.
Note: Council Special Reports are available for download from CFR's website, www.cfr.org.
For more information, email publications@cfr.org.